THE SUCCESS OF

the Navajo Arts and Crafts Enterprise

Other Books in the Success Series
Published by Walker and Company

The Success of Caroline Jones Advertising,
Inc.: An Advertising Success Story,
by Robert Fleming

The Success of Gordon H Chong + Associates:
An Architecture Success Story
by Steven A. Chin

The Success of Hispanic *Magazine:*
A Publishing Success Story,
by John García

THE SUCCESS OF

the Navajo Arts and Crafts Enterprise

A RETAIL SUCCESS STORY

LeNORA BEGAY TRAHANT

Photographs by Monty Roessel

WALKER AND COMPANY

NEW YORK

First published in the United States of America in 1996 by Walker
Publishing Company, Inc.

Published simultaneously in Canada by Thomas Allen & Son Canada,
Limited, Markham, Ontario

Library of Congress Cataloging-in-Publication Data
Trahant, LeNora Begay.
The success of the Navajo Arts and Crafts Enterprise : a retail
success story / LeNora Begay Trahant ; photographs by Monty Roessel.
          p.   cm.
Includes index.
Summary: A history of the Navajo business enterprise that
successfully markets tribal arts and crafts.
ISBN 0-8027-8336-8 (hc). — ISBN 0-8027-8337-6 (reinforced)
1. Navajo Arts and Crafts Enterprise—History—Juvenile
literature.   2. Navajo business enterprises—History—Juvenile
literature.   3. Navajo Indians—Economic conditions—Juvenile
literature.   4. Handicraft industries—Southwest, New—Juvenile
literature.   [1. Navajo Arts and Crafts Enterprise.   2. Handicraft
industries—Southwest, New.   3. Navajo Indians.   4. Indians of North
America—Southwest, New.]   I. Roessel, Monty, ill.   II. Title.
          E99.N3T73   1995
       381'.45745'089972—dc20   95-35464
                    CIP
                    AC

Printed in the United States of America

2   4   6   8   10   9   7   5   3   1

Contents

Foreword

We all know that in today's world, information is at a premium. Communication has taken on a life of its own as more and better technology becomes available to us. With these advances comes a responsibility, especially for those cultures and peoples whose past communications have been based in the oral tradition. Native Americans' information about themselves has either been passed down through the family, community, and tribe or been conveyed by nonnative people. This lack of direct information is important because there is a cultural perspective that can only be shared in a direct manner. For that reason, books like LeNora Begay Trahant's are a crucial part of this new tradition.

Little is known or understood about a tribe's growth and the growth of a tribe's enterprise from a Native perspective. Native American youth face a unique challenge as they grow up being part of two worlds. With that duality comes an obligation by their families, communities, and tribes to help them make sense of their uncommon world. *The Success of the Navajo Arts and Crafts Enterprise* serves as a strong image for both those worlds in that it carries on a cultural tradition and is a successful business.

As someone who was politically active in the 1960s, I also see in NACE the success that eluded many of us who were trying to form cooperatives of one kind or another at that time. The cooperative is based on communal ownership (rather than individual entrepreneurs), which is the basic tenet of the tribe itself. Documenting the history of a prosperous cooperative is not only historically important—so that we don't have to keep reinventing the wheel—but in NACE's case, that documentation is being written by a Native American, and that is invaluable.

—LaDonna Harris

Preface

Ya'at'eeh. My name is LeNora Begay Trahant. I am *Tachii'ni* (my mother's clan is the Red Running Into Water People) and born for the *To'-dich'ii'niis* (or my father's clan, the Bitter Water People). The *Ta'nees-zah niis* (The Tangle People) are my grandfathers and *Kinyaa'aanniis* (The Towering House People) are my paternal grandfathers.

This is how I was taught to introduce myself. The lesson, I was told, is that a person who knows oneself is never alone. "Wherever you go, you will find relatives," my maternal grandparents often repeated to me and my siblings. "If you are not willing to know yourself, you will not only be lost but alone in this world."

I grew up in a very small Navajo community called Sawmill, Arizona. This community is nestled up against a forest on the Fort Defiance Plateau, about fifteen miles northwest of the Navajo Nation's capital of Window Rock, Arizona.

At an early age, I bonded with my grandparents in a very special way. *Shi Cheii* (my grandfather) and *Shi Masa'ni'* (my grandmother), are two of the most influential people in my life. They gave me a solid background. They taught me my language, my culture, and basically about who I am as a person. My own parents realized this and decided to allow me to live with my grandparents. And when I was ten, I was legally adopted by my maternal grandparents, Marie and Sam Billie. I remain, however, close to my natural parents, Raymond and Margaret Begay.

It was about that time when I began to realize that there were many dreams to capture in this lifetime. My grandfather, who was an active leader in the community, had great dreams for me.

First and most important, he insisted that the only way to make a decent living was to get an education. Even though he has been dead for more than a decade, I can still hear my grandfather saying, "Get your education my children. It's the only way to make a living in this world. I can only wonder now how much more I could have offered my family, my community, and my people, if I was educated in the white man's ways. But you have that opportunity. Please don't waste it."

Another individual who played a significant role in my life was a Navajo teacher who taught me that a woman has no limits when it comes to life challenges. Ernestine Bates Lopez (her name at the time) was more of a friend than an instructor. She was the perfect role model. She encouraged many Navajo students to be proud of their Navajo heritage. Mrs. Lopez died in 1994, but her teachings and dreams are being lived out by those who were influenced by her.

When I completed high school in 1978, I had many choices to make: Starting a family was out of the question; acquiring a job on the reservation was almost impossible; and just staying home would only be a waste of time. So, I chose to attend Yavapai Community College in Prescott, Arizona, located about 100 miles northwest of Phoenix, Arizona. There, I took all the required classes and took an interest in journalism and social work. I enjoyed writing from the start.

The field of journalism was new to me. Although I worked on the school newspaper in high school and continued to write news articles in college, it never occurred to me that journalism could be a career. At that time, there were very few Indian journalists. Our weekly tribal newspaper, the *Navajo Times,* was mostly written and edited by non-Indians. During spring and summer breaks, I worked for the *Navajo Times.* I began as a newspaper carrier, then ventured into the circulation department, and later began writing stories for the paper. In 1983 a new editor who pushed for and promoted Navajo writers came to the *Times.* I went to work for the paper as a reporter. I covered tribal government, tribal politics, tribal courts, and the Navajo-Hopi land dispute.

I also was there when the paper became a daily newspaper, *The Navajo Times Today*. In 1986, the newspaper was closed by then tribal chairman, Peter MacDonald, and I ended up in Denver, Colorado, writing and editing the National Indian Health Board newsletter.

In late 1988, I returned to the reservation to work for the Navajo Nation as the public information officer. In 1990, I joined two colleagues to start an independent newspaper on the Navajo reservation, *Navajo Nation Today*. I was the managing editor and co-owner, and I learned firsthand how difficult it is to start a business on the reservation. Currently, I write a column on American Indian issues for *The Salt Lake Tribune*. Without the examples and encouragement of the role models in my life, I may not have accomplished all that I have.

—Lenora Begay Trahant

I remember when I was in the fifth grade; my teacher asked the class to write an essay on a role model. After a long silence, a classmate sitting next to me, said, "we live in Many Farms, there are no role models here."

We spent the rest of the day talking about people we admired and people we looked up to. Sports heroes didn't count, though if they did my essay would have been easy—Johnny Bench. Famous people also didn't count, so I had to cross out Hubert Humphrey (as vice president of the United States he visited the Navajo Nation). The role models had to be alive so I couldn't write about the great Navajo, Chief Manuelito.

Our teacher urged us to look no further than our home. Finally, the light bulb clicked on inside my head and the image of my mother came to light. A true role model is hard to find, but not hard to keep. Too often, we look for someone who can impress our friends rather than someone who left an impression on us.

As I sat in that classroom, I remembered the story my mom told me about her high school guidance counselor telling her that the best she could look forward to was to get married and have her husband take care of her. If she was lucky, maybe she would work as a waitress. This was a period of termination, when the government was trying to "scrub the Indian white" and assimilate us. My mom just smiled and said thank you.

Today, she has a master's degree in education, has written no fewer than six books, and is a recognized leader in Indian education. What makes her my role model is not what she has accomplished but the way in which her accomplishments have been realized. I have never heard her say a bad word about anyone—even her former guidance counselor. Her success comes because she believes in herself. Her strength comes from being Navajo. It is that person I try to model myself after.

My parents instilled in me a great sense of pride in being Navajo. One of the reasons I am a photographer is because I am tired of outsiders stepping into my community and supposedly telling "our" story. It is time that Navajos tell their own story.

In a way, Navajo culture is also my role model. The history, both tragic and triumphant, sets an example for never giving up. Respect for elders and the young teaches compassion. And an understanding that the land is alive inspires us to be responsible.

I am half Navajo and half white. When I was growing up, kids used to tease me about being a "half-breed." It hurt. I used to come home crying. One day, my mother came home from work early and saw my sad face. I told her what had happened. I can still remember her advice: "You are what you believe you are, not what others say you are." From that day forward I was Navajo.

—Monty Roessel

THE **SUCCESS** OF

the Navajo Arts and Crafts Enterprise

A salesperson admires the craftsmanship in the NACE store.

Introduction

When ten-year-old Leighanne Damon enters the Navajo Arts and Crafts Enterprise store, she eagerly heads toward the glass counter that displays tribal crafts by the hundreds: beaded barrettes, silver and turquoise earrings, woven baskets, and hand-sewn dolls. Then she wanders throughout the store, carefully looking at the handmade clothes on racks, moccasins hanging on pegs, and traditional Navajo rugs on the walls. The rugs grab her attention.

"I wonder how long it takes to make rugs," Leighanne says. "I think it would be fun to make your own designs." She points to bundles of spun woolen yarn hanging on one wall and says, "You will need a lot of that to make a rug."

Every day many Navajos come to the Navajo Arts and Crafts Enterprise (NACE) to buy the raw materials needed to make rugs and jewelry. Some of these same people then sell their finished crafts back to NACE, where they are sold again to individuals like Leighanne.

To understand the story of the Navajo Arts and Crafts Enterprise, you must first learn a little about the Navajo people. Navajos call themselves *Dine'*, which means "the People" in their native language. The Navajo Nation is the largest Native American tribe in the United States, including approximately 220,000 members. Moreover, the Navajo population is growing at a rate of more than 2 percent every year.

Navajos live in an area reserved for them by the U.S. government in a

All of the NACE stores sell wool ready for weaving.

peace treaty of 1868. The United States promised that the Navajos could live on these lands forever, if the Navajo leaders promised to stop fighting with the U.S. army and the white settlers moving westward. These reserved lands are special to the Navajos, because they encompass what is called *Dine' Bikeyah*, which simply means "our land." Navajo tradition teaches that the People should live between the Four Sacred Mountains: Blanca Peak in Colorado; Mount Taylor near Grants, New Mexico; San Francisco Peaks near Flagstaff, Arizona; and Hesperus Peak north of Cortez, near Alamosa, Colorado. Most of what is now the reservation is within those sanctified boundaries.

The Navajo Nation stretches across 25,000 square miles—roughly the same size as the state of West Virginia. The Navajo Nation appears on maps in the area of the United States called the "Four Corners." The Navajos live in northeastern Arizona, northwestern New Mexico, southeastern Utah, and southwestern Colorado.

From their earliest contacts with first the Spanish and then other Europeans, the Navajos have been noted for their unique artistic talents. In fact, the word *Navajo* often appears in connection with various artworks: Navajo rugs, Navajo necklaces, and even a Navajo design.

The Navajos tell their own stories about how they learned these skills. Legend has it that Spider Woman—a holy being—taught the People to weave to protect them from cold and heat. Anthropologists say that Navajos learned the craft from their neighbors, the Pueblos. The Navajos and the anthropologists agree, however, that silversmithing was a craft learned from the Spanish when they came to the Southwest in the late fifteenth century.

The Navajo Arts and Crafts Enterprise sits in a brick, rectangular building on Navajo Highway 264 in the tribal capital of Window Rock, Arizona. During the summer months, tour buses stop at the building nearly every day. Hundreds of tourists come into the store to buy authentic Navajo and other American Indian jewelry, rugs, and baskets. Similar NACE stores in Alamo and Gallup, New Mexico, and in Chinle and Cameron, Arizona, serve different areas of the reservation.

Hundreds of different pieces of artwork and crafts are on display at the

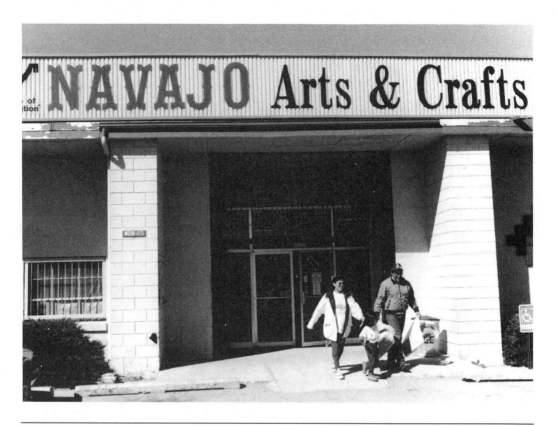

The Navajo Arts and Crafts Enterprise in Window Rock, Arizona, is a popular stop for artists and tourists.

NACE building in Window Rock: silver, gold, and turquoise jewelry; colorful woven rugs and belts; sandpaintings; moccasins; deerskin and other animal hides; blankets; traditional-style clothing; pottery; wedding baskets; kachina dolls; and many more. Modern items are for sale, too: T-shirts, and tapes of powwows, Native American Church songs, Navajo songs, and music from other Indian tribes. As noted earlier, the store also sells raw materials and supplies to craftspeople.

Throughout its existence, NACE has promoted and provided many jobs for Navajos skilled at handicrafts. And many people living in the Navajo Nation today earn a living making or selling crafts. Come meet some of the artists and businesspeople who make the Navajo Arts and Crafts Enterprise a success.

Head silversmith Howard Begay works in the window at the main store in Window Rock.

· 1 ·

History of the
Navajo Arts and Crafts Enterprise

No one knows exactly when Navajos began working with silver. The Spanish governor Fernando de Chacon wrote about the Navajos in a letter on July 15, 1795: "They have increased their horse herds considerably; they sow much and on good fields; they work their wool with more delicacy and taste than the Spaniards. Men as well as women go decently clothed; and their captains are rarely seen without silver jewelry."

Thus sometime before 1795 Navajos probably learned the craft from the Spanish *plateros* (silversmiths) who settled in villages in the upper Rio Grande valley of New Mexico—the southeastern edge of what is now the Navajo Reservation. But some experts disagree, and insist that the Navajos did not learn the craft until after the middle of the nineteenth century, although they had been wearing silver for many years.

Despite the conflicting theories about *when* Navajos started silversmithing, the fact is that Navajos excel at this craft. Today, there are thousands of Navajo silversmiths. And new techniques and tools are being used by some Navajos to make other types of metal and stones—including gold, diamond, lapis, and ruby—into jewelry that is uniquely Navajo.

The trading of Navajo crafts was started by white traders who came to the reservation after 1900. They came for the rare jewelry and rugs (then called Navajo blankets) that many people in the East were interested in buying.

A SILVERSMITHING FAMILY

Justin Wilson is a forty-six-year-old Navajo silversmith. He lives on a dirt road some two miles west of the Nazlini Trading Post and about thirty miles west of Window Rock, the capital of the Navajo Nation.

Justin's three-bedroom mobile home doubles as his workshop. He shares the house with his wife, Eunice, two daughters, and three granddaughters. A few feet from his home, there is another house where his son lives with his young family. This setting could be considered a traditional Navajo camp, because the Wilson family live in an isolated cluster of homes and all the neighbors are relatives. The area is on a high plateau, surrounded by red rocks, sagebrush, piñon, and juniper trees.

Before Justin began silversmithing, he worked at a sawmill in another reservation town. The salary was not enough to support his family of five. So he decided to move back to his family's traditional area and help his neighbors build a Full Gospel of Pentecostal Church.

"We moved out here in 1974 and built the church," Wilson says with a serious look as he pulls up a chair next to his wife. "My children were very small, and I didn't have much to look forward to because of the limited money. I began praying, and one night I had this dream. There was a tree stump, and on it were tools of all sorts, turquoise and various types of stones, and silver." He thought about his dream—and his nephew who made jewelry.

"I had the same dream one more time before I decided that my dreams were telling me something," Justin recalls. "I wanted to make this a reality, so I visited my nephew. Two hours later, we drove to Gallup, and the store owner there had enough confidence in me to give me a discount on the tools and supplies I needed to start off. He sold me a fifteen-dollar tool kit, put in some silver and tur-

quoise, and told me that I could pay him off when I made the jewelry."

For three years, Justin made simple pieces of jewelry, learning the fundamentals of his craft. He hammered and soldered the silver until the turquoise stones fit just right. Then, when his work became good enough, he started selling pieces of jewelry directly to Indian jewelry stores.

When Justin was working at the mill, Eunice had made extra money by weaving and selling Navajo rugs. But soon after her husband started his new career, she quit making the rugs and learned how to make silver jewelry too.

"It takes a lot of time and effort to weave a Navajo rug," says Eunice. "It took me about four weeks to finish a medium-sized rug, because I did it the traditional way: gathering special plants and herbs to make the dyes, shearing the wool off the sheep, washing and spinning it into yarn, setting up the loom, and finally weaving it into a rug. I started to help out my husband and saw that he was spending only two days working on a bracelet or something, then it would be ready to sell. My rug took days and weeks to complete in order to get any money. This is when I decided to work with him."

Workshops are scattered throughout the Wilsons' home. On the covered front porch there is a buffing machine for cleaning and polishing finished pieces of jewelry. In the short hall leading to the bedrooms there is a wooden worktable where Justin crafts his jewelry. Various types of tools lie about, along with a torch, pieces of turquoise, and silver. What used to be the second bathroom is now an additional workshop. A grinding machine and thousands of raw turquoise stones are scattered over a tabletop that sits on what was once a sink. In Eunice and Justin's bedroom, another workshop has been squeezed into the home. Eunice works on her jewelry here.

Business is good. The Wilson family is planning to expand: An old trailer-house outside is being reconstructed to replace the workshops in the house.

Justin, who prefers to speak in Navajo, says it's not that difficult to craft silver. He walks over to his worktable and lifts a partially finished necklace—a piece of silver waiting for just the right turquoise stones. "You have to learn how to work with the silver first," Justin says as he holds up several thin strips of silver to show what the raw metal looks like. The heat from a gasoline torch melts down the raw silver and makes it easy to bend and twist the metal into the desired shape.

Justin then points out a tiny cup-shaped housing. This is the silver that holds a turquoise stone tightly in place. He explains that to create the necklace, which will have dozens of stone clusters, he must "grind down hundreds of turquoise stones to fit into these small holes [of the housing]. Grinding the stones is the most difficult part, because it takes a long time and you have to make them fit just right."

Large chunks of raw turquoise are lying on the bathroom tabletop and are ready to be cut into smaller pieces. Then the stones will be ground into small round or oval jewels, and finally polished to create a glossy look.

Setting the turquoise into the silver is the last step before the jewelry is cleaned and buffed so it sparkles. The stones are cushioned with a pinch of sawdust in the housing, which acts as a soft barrier to keep the stones from breaking or cracking. The polished turquoise stones are placed into the housing, and the housing sides are bent toward the stone so that they act like a clamp.

Justin is proud of his and his family's work. He points to a huge poster on his wall showing Miss Navajo wearing bracelets, necklaces, and pins. Then he says, "We made this set for her."

Each bracelet made by the Wilsons uses about two hundred turquoise stones and requires some ten hours of labor. Necklaces take longer because of the sheer num-

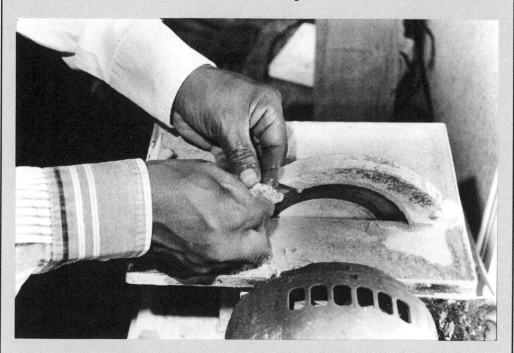

Cutting the turquoise to fit is just one of the many steps in making fine silver jewelry.

ber of silver housings needed to hold clusters of stones.

Two of the Wilsons' three children have learned the craft too. By the time they graduated from high school, they had developed their own style.

"We were looking for our own specialty, and we found it," Eunice says proudly. "The cluster work has really paid off. That's all we make now, because of the demand for it. It is a lot of work, but it's something that we are recognized for in this business."

One of the Wilsons' first clients for their cluster jewelry was the Navajo Arts and Crafts Enterprise in Window Rock. Every other week, Eunice and her daughter Justina take their creations to sell at NACE.

"The Navajo Arts and Crafts have been buying our jewelry regularly because it has become popular among their customers," Eunice says. "They tell us our jewelry is selling, so we keep coming back to them."

"We usually sell my necklaces to NACE for about $200 or $250 at a wholesale price," Justin says. "When I get special orders from individuals, we sell [them] for more."

"A person could make about five or six bracelets in a week," Eunice says. "That's if you don't do anything else. If you concentrate on a project and spend time on it, you can make as much as $2,000 in a week's time."

The traders were settlers who made a living bartering with Navajos, Zunis, Hopis, and other tribes, and who promoted silver and turquoise jewelry in particular. One trader, Joel Higgins Adams, saw the potential for long-term profits and opened a trading post in Gallup, New Mexico, in 1910. He hired silversmiths to make what he called "fancy, lightweight jewelry." Joel advertised his creations by mailing out thousands of brochures across the country. Soon there were thousands of silversmiths, mostly Navajos, employed in Gallup.

The Navajo government was organized in the 1930s. Most of its early work centered on oil, gas, and other natural resources. After noticing the problem with fake Indian jewelry, tribal officials encouraged Indian schools to teach young people silversmithing.

In 1940, the Navajo Nation started the Navajo Arts and Crafts Guild in Fort Wingate, New Mexico. Ambrose Roanhorse, a Navajo silversmith, was named the director. One year later, the guild expanded across the reservation.

The guild's purpose was to increase tribal income and sell Navajo crafts across the country. One of its first managers was anthropologist John Adair, who wrote: "The tourist market is purposely avoided, as it does not yield as high a return per man-hours as the more exclusive stores and shops. During the first two years of its existence, the guild has never been able to fill all of its orders—proof that there is a good market for the very finest type of Navajo handicrafts."

The guild continued to grow steadily. Navajos who were unable to obtain jobs on the reservation found they could earn a living making crafts. Most of the jobs on the reservation were—and still are—limited to government agencies such as the U.S. Indian Health Service and the Bureau of Indian Affairs, or in the tribal government. There are only a handful of privately owned companies.

In 1972, the guild became the Navajo Arts and Crafts Enterprise. This was not just a change of name but a fundamental change in the structure and nature of the crafts operation. Whereas the guild had been a tribal department that was confined by many tribal regulations, the enterprise could function more independently—with no direct involvement by tribal politicians. A board of directors was appointed to act as a buffer between the enterprise and the tribal government. Peter MacDonald, who was tribal chairman at the time, oversaw these developments and conceived the idea for the enterprise to mass-produce Navajo jewelry—much like the earlier operation of Joel Higgins Adams.

One hundred Navajos were hired as silversmiths. "The idea . . . was to

Salesclerk Alisa Litson displays traditional Navajo jewelry.

make millions of dollars," says Raymond Smith, the current general manager of NACE. "On paper, the plan looked good, and it showed it would be a viable business."

During the mid-1970s, Indian silver jewelry was extremely popular. Movie stars and other celebrities wore silver bracelets and rings, as well as

14

belts adorned with silver. Large national retailers like Sears Roebuck and Montgomery Ward bought large quantities of Navajo jewelry.

NACE hired managers familiar with assembly line operations to keep the silversmiths on a production schedule.

"One thing led to another, and the quality of the jewelry went down," Raymond Smith says. "[The managers] only cared about how much jewelry

Raymond Smith helps customers in the Window Rock store.

was being produced. As a result, the silversmiths got sloppy with their work. Later the price of silver began to rise tremendously."

In one attempt to benefit from the exploding market, the enterprise accepted a large order from a store in New York City—but could not produce enough pieces to fill it. Instead of relaying this message back to the department store, the managers bought huge amounts of jewelry from the traders in Gallup. They were desperate to fill the order.

"The department store had placed the order for quality Indian jewelry, but they found out it was junk jewelry," says Raymond Smith. "The jewelry was sent back to NACE, and that's when the enterprise took a nosedive. It lost its accountability, its integrity, and just about everything."

What's more, the price of silver continued to rise. By the early 1980s, silver prices rose from four dollars to fifty dollars an ounce. This forced many jewelry traders—both off and on the reservation—out of the business.

After losing about $1 million, the tribe pared down its jewelry operation. NACE's current chairman of the board, Frank Chee Willeto, vividly recalls discussions about closing down. Instead, the board decided to change course. Most of the general managers who had run NACE were non-Indian traders or businesspeople. But the board now realized they needed a Navajo who understood the tribe and the jewelry business.

It was 1977, and Raymond Smith, a former member of the Navajo Tribal Council, was enjoying his retirement. Members of the board of directors for the Navajo Arts and Crafts Enterprise asked him to take over the wobbly enterprise. "They came down to my house in Lupton [Arizona]," he recalls. "I told them they had a lot of people with MBA degrees to pick from. But they insisted on someone who had experience with the tribal government."

Frank Chee, a silversmith and who was then a council delegate from Pueblo Pintado, New Mexico, says that Raymond was reluctant to accept the job right away. "He wanted to take a look at NACE's financial report first. He came back to us later and told us we were in a big mess. We had to convince him to help us. The task of turning the business around was a challenge."

Raymond says he consulted with his family—and then decided to give it a try.

Raymond Smith works behind the scenes at NACE.

· 2 ·

Stability in Leadership, Owner, and Team

Raymond Smith accepted the challenge of turning the Navajo Arts and Crafts Enterprise around, but it wasn't easy.

"During the first year that Mr. Smith got on board, NACE barely made it," says Frank Chee. "But we were headed in the right direction. As the years went by, things started to improve. He has been with us for fifteen years now—working [the enterprise] from a deficit to a moneymaking business."

Years of hard work, sound management skills, and the hiring of knowledgeable employees has brought NACE back into profitability. Also, the price of silver has dropped to about four dollars an ounce, making it less costly for the artisans to produce the products NACE sells.

From the very beginning, Raymond sought experienced, dependable employees who would help build a team. "Number one was getting salespeople who are honest and want to help the enterprise. The accounting section needed to be fully revamped. The reputation for NACE quality needed to be restored. Knowing that history can repeat itself, we have stressed the importance of quality from all the people we do business with."

Today, there are two employees at NACE's Window Rock establishment who make certain that the quality of each rug or piece of jewelry is first-rate. Their names are Kent Walker and Alice Hawthorne.

As a sales manager and buyer, Kent Walker does business with people from all over the reservation, who come to his small office every day to sell their handicrafts. This office has a small couch, a chair, a wooden bookshelf,

19

RAYMOND SMITH

The office of the Navajo Arts and Crafts Enterprise's general manager is located at the end of a short hallway past the secretary's desk and accounting offices. There, Raymond Smith keeps busy looking over a report that he's preparing to give to the Navajo Nation Council in the next few days. It is one of the annual reports he is required to submit to the tribal council about the progress of NACE.

His desk is cluttered with stacks of documents, files, and office supplies. Several file cabinets, two office chairs, and a short brown couch comprise the rest of the office furniture. Decorating the walls are paintings and colorful Navajo rugs. Raymond Smith has been in this same office for fifteen years and has no plans of leaving soon.

The seventy-five-year-old manager grew up in Lupton, Arizona, and continues to live there with his wife, Lucille. He attended several nearby schools: St. Michael's Catholic School, Fort Defiance's Bureau of Indian Affairs School, and Rehoboth Mission School. He graduated from Sanders High School and immediately enrolled with the U.S. Marines. He left for service right after graduation.

"Before I left for the marines, I had thought about opening up some kind of business near my home," Raymond remembers. "In those days [early 1940s] there were no nearby stores to shop for groceries or anything."

After learning that it was nearly impossible to open up a business on the reservation without a considerable amount of money and land to build on, Raymond decided to work for the marine base in Barstow, California, to save up enough money to pursue his dream.

He returned to Lupton after saving enough money to open a small grocery. This store was located near Highway 66, where many travelers stopped for gas and groceries. But when Interstate 40 was built, his business dropped considerably and he had to shut it down.

It was time for Raymond Smith to look for another job. Several members of his community asked him to run for a seat in the Navajo Tribal Council (the name was changed to Navajo Nation Council in 1991) to represent the surrounding communities of Lupton, Houck, and Sanders. He was elected and served on that council for twenty years. During this time, he became chairman of the council's Budget and Finance Committee, a powerful committee that makes decisions on where to spend the tribe's money.

In the mid-1970s, Raymond decided he was going to retire and spend more time with his family. But only a few years later, he was approached by NACE's board of directors, who asked him to come to work for them.

"I knew it was going to be a great challenge, because I was fully aware of what was happening to this business," he remembers. "It was in need of money as well as a new management team. I wanted to prove that an Indian, a Navajo, can run the business successfully, so I took the job."

NACE has thrived under Raymond Smith's leadership. He attributes his business sense to his years in tribal politics serving on the Budget and Finance Committee. He also takes pride in the employees who have stayed with him during the tough times.

Today, Raymond handles all reports, legislation that need tribal council approval, loan agreements between the tribe and banks, and confirmation of new board members. He sits on numerous associations such as the Arizona Native American Economic Coalition. He also meets regularly with the NACE board, tribal officials, and local craftspeople. "All in all it's a very diversified type of an operation. My job takes me to many places."

two file cabinets, and a desk. High on the wall above him is a small shelf that holds two black radios.

At about ten o'clock every morning, Kent turns up the volume to the radio station playing country and western music, picks up the telephone, and calls the station to tape a brief message: "Good morning, the silver prices today are $4.31 an ounce, and gold is $361 an ounce," he says while playing his improvised background music. Kent then adds a minute or two of promotion for hot items at NACE and reminds customers about the business hours.

"My main purpose here is to increase sales," Kent says. "In order to do that, I have to be very informed and knowledgeable about the products I'm purchasing. I would like to save about 5 percent in my purchasing efforts [purchase prices], which would translate into about 25 percent increase in sales. Because I have not been here long enough, I have not achieved that goal—yet."

Knowledgeable salespeople make the difference for NACE customers.

Negotiating with and purchasing from craft makers are vital to the enterprise's success. Kent needs to make sure NACE buys the crafts at a fair price so the craft makers will keep selling to the enterprise, which makes a profit when it sells these crafts to its customers.

Unlike other employees, Kent has a contract that is reviewed by the board of directors every year. There is much pressure to keep working hard. "My contract was just renewed," he says with a grin.

Every week, Kent goes on a shopping spree. "My budget varies, anywhere from $5,000 to $1,500 per week, depending on the cash flow situation. This takes care of about thirty different vendors a week. I often limit this to approximately $500 per person." How much he spends depends on how much NACE sold the week before.

23

KENT WALKER

This forty-eight-year-old sales manager and buyer was born and raised in Tuba City, Arizona. (Tuba City is on the far western edge of the Navajo Reservation, near the Grand Canyon.) Kent attended and graduated from Phoenix Indian School, a government boarding school in Phoenix, Arizona. So he spent much of his childhood away from home and in the city.

But during the summer vacation months, Kent returned home to Tuba City to help his parents with their daily chores raising livestock and herding sheep.

During these long summer days herding sheep, Kent daydreamed about running his own business on the reservation. Few entrepreneurs on the reservation have enough money to start—and develop—their own companies. Kent did start a construction company at one time, but it survived only three years.

In addition to trying his hand at business, Kent worked for the tribe for many years. He had jobs working directly with people as well as management positions. He once served as a mediator and translator for the Navajo-Hopi Land Office, and for about fifteen years he was employed by a legal services program as a tribal court advocate both in Window Rock and Tuba City. On the side, Kent worked as a silversmith for more than twenty years.

Kent still calls Tuba City his home. Because it's a four-hour drive to work, he stays in an apartment in Window Rock from Monday through Friday. But he spends weekends with his wife and daughter in Tuba City.

Kent speaks fluent Navajo and English. This is a crucial skill for someone working with Navajo people, because many do not speak English. And the majority of craftspeople doing business with NACE prefer to speak their own language.

Kent still has hopes to run his own business someday. He has taken several college courses in business administration to prepare himself. He is thinking of venturing into the jewelry business, like many of the people with whom he works. But for now, he is concentrating on his job with NACE.

At NACE, the purchasing of crafts is done according to a fixed schedule. For example, on Mondays, Wednesdays, and Fridays its Window Rock establishment will buy from craftspeople who make silver and turquoise jewelry. In most cases, the artisan is paid on the spot, after both parties reach an agreement on prices. (A few handicrafts are carried in NACE stores on consignment. This means that NACE will pay the artisan only for those items that sell and may return unsold items.)

Once the items are purchased, they are repriced and placed in the show-

Kent Walker inspects a silversmith's jewelry before making an offer.

cases at NACE for sale to the public. Because NACE is competing against the hundreds of arts and crafts stores in the area (especially those in Gallup, New Mexico, which is within thirty miles of Window Rock), it is forced to advertise its products.

Kent Walker works with an annual marketing budget of $70,000 to $80,000. Approximately $65,000 is used for NACE's advertising campaign. Kent focuses on ads in local and regional radio stations, newspapers, and magazines. "Locally, I think radio is by far the best way to reach our customers," he says, "because it allows us to advertise in both the Navajo and English languages. Many of our customers are tribal members, so we have to reach out to them in their own language. We do place ads in magazines and newspapers throughout the country in our attempt to bring in the tourists."

Kent travels all over the United States to sell NACE products. He especially likes to participate in art shows, where he can meet and make contacts with other Indian jewelry dealers in the country. According to Kent, the shows are "a great way to expose our Navajo jewelry and rugs. If the customers don't come to us, we're going to go out to them." He usually takes along one or two artists to make a rug or jewelry in front of an audience. NACE attends at least four art shows every year in Pasadena, California; Houston, Texas; or Denver, Colorado.

When Kent Walker is traveling or at the NACE branch stores, Alice Hawthorne is the person in charge.

Alice started working at the Navajo Arts and Crafts Enterprise when her children were old enough to go to school—that was more than twelve years ago. She started as an entry-level salesperson and was later promoted to inventory clerk and then supervisor, and is now the manager of the Window Rock store.

Alice has many responsibilities. She oversees sixteen employees, buys merchandise, and is in charge of consignment sales. She is also NACE's rug expert and travels around the country to demonstrate Navajo rug weaving at art shows.

Alice learned how to identify the best rugs when she was making her own. Since she was widowed when her oldest daughter was two, she depended on her rug-weaving skills to support her family. She later remarried but continued to weave as a way to bring in extra income for her growing family. Alice speaks of weaving as a way of life for her mother, grandmother, and herself. She brings this knowledge and experience with her when she's

Alice Hawthorne carefully inspects each rug she buys to be sure it meets NACE's standards for quality.

ALICE HAWTHORNE

Alice Hawthorne, the manager of NACE's Window Rock store, grew up among the hills, red rocks, sagebrush, and pine trees near Houck, Arizona. (Houck is located in the southwest portion of the Navajo Reservation, about thirty miles south of Window Rock.) "I spent my childhood herding sheep," she says. "I was raised by my mother and grandmother—both were weavers. That is where I learned the art of weaving. Every-thing from shearing the wool off the sheep to dying the yarn, spinning and carding the wool, and weaving it into rugs."

Alice attended a small Catholic school in Sanders, Arizona, which is about fifteen miles southwest of her home in Houck. She later transferred to a boarding school in Fort Wingate, New Mexico, where she received her high school education.

At the age of fifteen, Alice started working at a restaurant in Gallup as a waitress. The restaurant had a small shop in the corner where Indian jewelry and crafts were sold. The owners decided to expand the shop and asked her to help sell the jewelry and other crafts.

Now in her mid-fifties, Alice recalls: "This is where I learned many skills, such as dealing and communicating with the customers, and how to sell the jewelry [pieces] by talking about how they are made," she says. "About this time, I started wearing a lot of jewelry. I still wear jewelry. I love it."

Alice proudly displays the silver and turquoise rings, earrings, necklace, and bracelets she is wearing.

Alice quit her sales job when she got married. She raised three girls and two boys. Her focus was on being a mother and caretaker of her own sheep, cattle, and horses. When time allowed, Alice worked on her own rugs. Thus she was carrying on the family tradition of raising sheep and rug weaving.

"One day," she says with a chuckle, "[after] watching all these non-Indians making money on Indian jewelry, I decided that I can do that too. So I put my weaving aside and purchased all the necessary tools and materials [to become a silversmith]. Yes, it took time to learn, but I was determined to do it."

After her children got a little older, Alice began working as an arts and crafts instructor at the Bureau of Indian Affairs School at Fort Wingate. "I taught high school students, mostly females, rug and basket weaving." She then quit her job to care for her seventh child.

Alice was first hired by NACE as a salesperson at a branch store in Allentown, near her home in Three Hogans. This store was closed when the enterprise was losing money. But when NACE was looking for a buyer/inventory clerk in the late 1970s, Alice was rehired by general manager Raymond Smith and has been at the Window Rock store ever since. She makes the commute from home, which is approximately ten miles east of Houck.

Alice says the stability Raymond Smith brought to the company is the greatest factor in the improvement of NACE. "We have had many general managers who came with their own ideas and some who were not very effective," she notes. "We had non-Indians as general managers who were unfamiliar with the arts and crafts business. When Mr. Smith came on board, there were improvements all the way around. We have set out many goals, and many of them have been accomplished. He encourages all the staff members to work as a team. He communicates well with employees and the board of directors. We all have to work together. Together we sacrifice a lot of our own time to keep this business running smoothly. That's what it takes. You have to be dedicated, work hard, and get along with people."

All of Alice's children are adults now. All are accomplished silversmiths—although only one daughter earns a living from her craft. The others have jobs with the tribe and know that if they should get laid off, they can always go back to arts and crafts.

Alice is very proud of her accomplishments. She has taught rug-weaving courses at Navajo Community College and many other schools across the reservation. In November of 1993, she was interviewed by weatherman Spencer Christian of ABC's *Good Morning America* about her weav-

ing skill. "I was very honored to be on national television doing what I like best.

"I have always been interested in arts and crafts," Alice says. "The people I deal with every day are very creative. There's always something new to look forward to. It is from this great interest in people and their artwork that I learned how to make pottery and how to weave baskets. You have to actually learn to do these things in order to really talk about what it is you're selling. It is very important to know what you're selling to your customers. This makes it easier to sell a product."

Alice plans to continue to teach rug weaving well into her retirement years. "I really enjoy teaching those who are interested in making rugs."

buying a rug. She inspects each rug thoroughly, looking at every strand of yarn. Only after she knows every thread in the rug does she begin negotiating on a price with the weaver. NACE advertises its Navajo rugs to be 100 percent wool. Therefore, Alice must make sure the rug fits the bill.

"A good-quality rug is determined by its tightness, if it's high-graded wool, and if it is made of natural dyes," she says, pointing to different rugs

Secretary, Velda Anderson (left) helps Alice Hawthorne get through her always-busy days at NACE.

on the wall of the Window Rock store. "I look at how a rug is woven, and how close the warps are, and then I determine what kind of rug it is by its design."

Alice believes the interest in the traditional patterns will never fade, although new weaves with pastel colors are coming from younger weavers.

NAVAJO WEAVER

A wooden loom with only a few strands of woolen yarn in each corner stands near the entrance to Betty Clyde's five-room house. The strands are the remains of a handwoven Navajo rug that she completed a few days ago.

"I sold the rug already," Betty says in Navajo. She does not speak English, although she understands it. "Now it's time to start another one."

Betty is a woman in her late sixties who lives near the small community of Pine Springs, Arizona, just off Interstate 40. She makes rugs for a living.

She grew up at a time when most women were taught how to weave a rug by their mothers or grandmothers. In the Navajo legends, the art of weaving was taught to Changing Woman by Spider Woman. Through Changing Woman weaving was passed on to the Navajos. Spider Woman told Changing Woman that if this art is passed on, the Navajos would have clothes to protect them from the weather.

Betty Clyde heard these stories when she was growing up. "It's a way of life for me," she explains. "Most young women and men in those days were told to herd sheep. I watched my mother weave rugs at home in the evenings. I didn't have to take any lessons or anything like that. Just watched how it was done and picked it up from there."

Betty has a large family: eight daughters, two sons, and twenty-three grandchildren. They all live close to her; several of her children's homes surround her family hogan.

The rug she just sold measured five feet long and four feet wide. It had wide black, white, and red stripes and large simple geometrical designs inside its border. She sold the rug for $700 to Griswolds Trading Post near Window Rock. She wanted to sell it to the Navajo Arts and Crafts Enterprise, where she normally goes, but the rug expert was not in town that particular day. "I needed to get some extra money right away, and I didn't want to wait another day. It takes time to go out there."

Betty started taking her rugs to

Betty and one of her grandsons check on the sheep they raise.

Betty Clyde at her loom.

NACE several years ago when she became familiar with the company's guidelines for buying rugs. "I know very well that they expect the best-quality rugs. The person who buys these rugs inspects them very carefully. I think that is good."

Betty says she stopped weaving when her children were young but began weaving again about twelve years ago when the family needed extra money to buy cloth-ing. "After selling a couple of them, I decided to continue because it was a good way to bring in extra money for my family," Betty says. "It's a lot of work, but I enjoy doing it. Not only to help support my family but also to keep this tradition alive. I think it's very important for the *Dine'* to hold on to some of their traditional ways. Our cultural ways are what makes us *Dine'*, with unique skills and beliefs."

At the urging of Betty, two of

her eldest daughters have learned to weave. Acquiring the skill takes a lot of practice and patience. It requires about three to five weeks to finish a rug—longer if you decide to do the entire process yourself: gathering the herbs and plants used to dye the wool, shearing the sheep, cleaning the sheep hair, and spinning it to make the yarn thinner so you can weave a tight rug.

But in the modern world, many Indian arts and crafts dealers sell ready-made woolen yarn in a variety of colors. This makes the job easier for Betty and other rug weavers.

"I purchase my yarn at the Arts and Crafts [NACE] now," Betty says. "They sell their yarn for about $2.65 or $2.90 a bundle. It saves a lot of time, but sometimes I have to respin it once more to thin it out."

Betty says most of her customers are interested in thin and tightly woven rugs. "They like to use them to hang on their walls or to cover furnishings," she says. "What they use it for depends on the type of rug, too—the patterns on the rugs, the size of the rug, and how well it is made."

The Navajo Arts and Crafts Enterprise sends Betty to art shows to demonstrate weaving. On her most recent trip, to Tucson, Arizona, Betty met a lot of people from all over the world. "They have a lot of questions to ask of me," she reports. "I enjoy going on these trips. It's a good time to meet people and show them my weaving.

"One thing I learned that was interesting is that Anglos and other tribes have picked up this weaving. I was told that there are classes now a person can take to learn to weave. I think it's sad to see others take our artwork and make it theirs. I believe we, Navajos, must teach our children. I hope it [the tradition of weaving] doesn't die out. Our grandchildren must continue learning from us. It is very important to keep it alive."

Betty says 1980 was her most productive year: She wove seventeen rugs. Nowadays it's hard to keep up that pace, but she still

> keeps busy with it.
>
> "I think rug weaving as an art will continue for as long as we [*Diné*] are here on this earth," Betty says. "But if we forget the history and all the legends that go with it, it will just be another moneymaking venture."

Throughout the years, Alice has met many rug weavers. She says most of them are excellent, but some take shortcuts to finish faster. She often refuses to buy the quick-turn rugs and even passes on beautiful rugs because of the content. "A lot of weavers nowadays try to get away with a little and experiment with mixed yarn—cotton and nylon warps," she says. "If I don't want to buy a certain rug, I tell them what is wrong with it. These rugs might be curling up on the sides, or they might be uneven. I measure the sides to make sure they are even. If they're not, the tension was too tight during the weaving process."

During her negotiations with the weavers, Alice follows a simple routine: "I usually ask them what [price] they want for it first to give them the chance to make their pitches. If weavers have good business sense, they would consider the going prices and give me a price I would be comfortable with. But if they quote me a price that is too high, I try to get them to lower [it]. . . . Sometimes this is when I let them know what might be wrong with the rug. . . . When a person comes in with a rug that is good, not excellent, and they want a high price for it, there is usually something wrong. Either they're just testing the waters, or they are unaware of the going rates.

"I always try to be up front and fair with these people, because I generally know what type of workmanship is involved. I have a firm idea of [the

Different colored yarns make the rug patterns beautiful.

cost of] the raw materials and approximately how much time is spent on [a rug]. In addition, I know how much a trader in Gallup might give for such a rug."

It is tough for Alice to reject some weavers. There are always a few people who come in determined to sell their rugs despite NACE's policy of buying only pure wool. "They get very defensive and angry. They feel that because NACE is owned by the tribe, we are obligated to buy all types of rugs from Navajo weavers. You've got to stand your ground and let them know what you expect," she says.

Some weavers say they will just go to town and sell their rug to a trader in Gallup. In Gallup, traders will pay cash or cash plus groceries for a rug. But in Gallup, quality is not the issue it is at NACE.

Alice sometimes travels to the homes of weavers who specialize in hard-to-get rugs: those with special patterns or made from wool colored with natural dyes. She also buys directly from community governments, called chapters, where a co-op is set up to represent local artists.

Although there are many Navajo weavers, Alice says there is a shortage of very fine rugs. The most famous rug weavers do not like to sell to stores, because they can make more money selling directly to individuals themselves. "They have to sell it wholesale to NACE," she explains, "so we can sell it for a reasonable price."

A high-quality rug adorns a wall in the Gallup store.

RUG PATTERNS

Before starting to weave a rug, a Navajo weaver seeks out plants and herbs that will dye the wool into many colors. She then prepares the wool by washing, dyeing, and drying out the bundles; brushing and carding out the wool into small fluffy rolls; and finally spinning the wool into thin strings of yarn.

A loom is set up with warps strung lengthwise from top to bottom. The weaver begins at the bottom by stringing the yarn through each warp thread. Each row of weaving is threaded across the loom from left to right. A design begins to take shape when the weaver begins to change the colors of the yarn. Sometimes a design is not apparent until she finishes a border about two to three

Buying wool that's already dyed speeds up the rug-making process.

inches from the bottom of the rug.

The patterns and designs on Navajo rugs are classified into four major styles: Two Grey Hills, Storm Pattern, Yei-bi-chai, and Ganado Red.

The Two Grey Hills rugs are the finest. They are made of natural wool in white, brown, gray, and black, and usually have an intricate geometric design with a border. Storm Pattern rugs are characterized by steplike lines that start in a triangle and end at each of the four corners. They are generally red, black, gray, and white. Yei-bi-chai rugs are more colorful, portraying several Yeis, or Navajo deities, dancing or standing. Ganado Red rugs normally have a deep red background surrounded by geometric designs such as crosses and diamonds.

Besides rugs, Alice is responsible for purchasing and appraising jewelry, baskets, and other crafts. "When I find that some of the jewelry . . . is not fully completed or there is something wrong with it, I don't hesitate to

Popular silver pieces tempt buyers.

share my ideas or experience with them [the jewelry makers]. I usually tell them what types of tools or chemicals they might use to improve their work. You'd be surprised how fast they pick it up. They appreciate these tips," she says.

About twenty years ago, silversmiths were adding decorative silver leaves to their jewelry. That was followed by a trend of silver feathers and a spider-weblike design called dream catchers. Now those are all out of fashion. Today the more traditional styles are the most popular: large pieces of oval-shaped silver around a belt (a concho belt), and bracelets and necklaces that have turquoise stones embedded in them. "Big nugget bracelets and cluster-style jewelry with less stamping are in now," Alice says.

A customer admires the jewelry in the NACE showcase in Gallup, New Mexico.

In order to develop a career in any type of craft, a person must work hard, have patience, take risks, and be creative, Alice says. "You have to keep up with the current trends and fashions to tap into this very competitive market. I tell all my clients that it's important to be aware of what our customers demand."

Maria Mann is one of the few silversmiths on staff at NACE.

· 3 ·

How NACE Works

The Navajo Arts and Crafts Enterprise, under the direction of Raymond Smith, improved by hiring employees who were responsive to the changes and the new direction of the enterprise.

A handful of the employees he hired in the early days are still working for NACE: Alice Hawthorne, whom we met in chapter 2, salesclerk Lottie Nez, silversmith Howard Begay, salesclerk Bernard Kinlicheeni, and Russell Morgan, manager of the wholesale division (see chapter 4).

Lottie Nez has been a salesclerk at the NACE Window Rock store for about fifteen years. "People here are willing to work with me by taking time to help me improve my skills. I must say that I have personally benefited from all this. I have improved my communication skills by selling jewelry in the sales department," she says in the Navajo language. Lottie is in her early seventies. As an elder, she has earned the respect and trust of hundreds of regular customers. The majority of her customers are tribal employees and elderly Navajos who are interested in items used in cere-monies: wedding baskets, moccasins, buckskins, sash belts, and Pendleton blankets. "Navajos love turquoise. It's one of their first personal purchases," she says.

Silversmith Howard Begay says NACE has made quality important again. "People know now that we only buy and sell quality jewelry. I have seen some of the best jewelry being sold from right here."

Howard and two other silversmiths sit in a workshop surrounded by tools and machines behind a large glass window near the cash register. How-

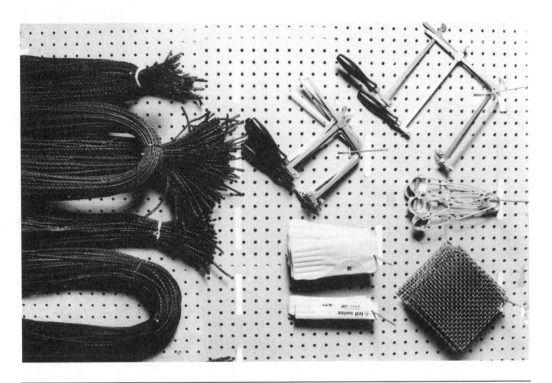

Everything an artisan needs can be bought from NACE.

ard and his coworkers make repairs on jewelry; they are the only full-time silversmiths at NACE in Window Rock. Occasionally, Howard travels to art shows to demonstrate his work.

NACE added a raw materials supply section in September 1985. Bernard Kinlicheeni, a salesclerk, was hired to stock silver, stones, wool, and tools to sell to silversmiths and rug weavers.

"Our main goal was to stock all our stores with quality materials that people can purchase here on the reservation," Bernard says. "Before that, people used to have to drive long distances just to get the supplies and materials they needed to do a project.

"As long as the enterprise has stability in its management, I think we will succeed and start competing with the traders in Gallup. There is a good cash

Being able to buy raw turquoise close to home helps the artists save time and money.

flow now. The general manager [Raymond Smith] knows what needs to be done. We just have to continue selling our high-quality handmade Indian crafts. We are capable of making millions of dollars. The business opportunity is there for us."

Business at the Navajo Arts and Crafts Enterprise improved considerably when it hired a *controller* to keep better track of the cash. Dennis Wyna, an MBA accounting graduate from the New Mexico Highlands University, had more than six years of experience working with accounting firms. Dennis was hired immediately after graduation by a Navajo-owned CPA (Certified Public Accountant) firm in Albuquerque, New Mexico. As a CPA, Dennis audited various Navajo tribal government programs.

Dennis was hired to manage NACE's accounting department in 1991.

"Our accounting system was very outdated," recalls Raymond Smith. "Everything was manual, and the accountants were always six to nine months behind. Now most of our operation is computerized, making it a lot easier to keep track of financial reports."

Several changes had to take place as Dennis began reorganizing and updating the accounting department. First, he arranged for an audit of the company and found ways to keep more accurate records. A computer system was in place at the time, but no one knew how to use it to its full capacity.

"I feel that NACE has come a long way since the time I first started working here," says Dennis, whose office wall is covered with several

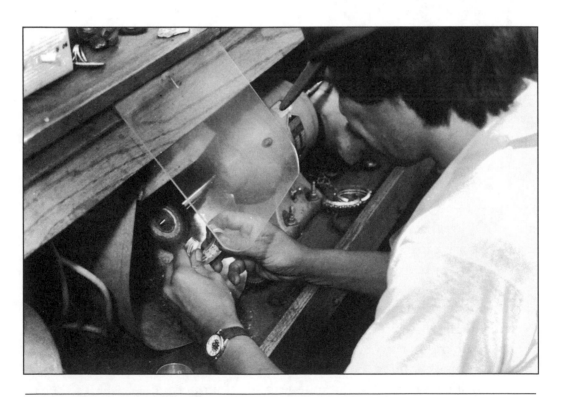

Customers can watch this silversmith repair a bracelet in the NACE shop.

DENNIS WYNA

The person who manages the money for the Navajo Arts and Crafts Enterprise is a professional accountant who has always been interested in working for Native American businesses. Dennis Wyna, thirty-five, is Hopi and Acoma Pueblo. He was born and raised on his father's land in the Acoma Pueblo, about fifty miles west of Albuquerque, New Mexico.

Dennis knew early on in high school that he was a good math student and wanted to have a career working with numbers. In 1977 he graduated from Grants High School, and in 1981 he earned his bachelor's degree in accounting from New Mexico Highlands University in Las Vegas, New Mexico. He went on to graduate school at the same university and was awarded a master's in business administration in 1983.

"I was fortunate enough to receive a grant," says Dennis in explaining how he was able to stay in school until he completed his graduate studies. He also took advantage of an accounting scholarship from the American Institute of Accountants.

"My first job, right out of college, was with Sloan and Company, a Navajo-owned CPA firm in Albuquerque," Dennis says. He worked there for three years as an auditor. "I had the opportunity to work with Peat Marwick and Maine Company, one of the big CPA firms."

Dennis then relocated to Shiprock, New Mexico, to work for the Navajo Engineering and Construction Authority Company, where he headed the company's accounting department for three years. "From there, I've had the opportunity to move to Window Rock, where I am presently with the Navajo Arts and Crafts Enterprise."

He lives in Gallup, New Mexico, about twenty-five miles east of Window Rock.

"I've worked with Native American businesses most of my career, mostly Navajos," Dennis says. "I've always been treated very well." But along the way, Dennis has learned a valuable lesson about working with Navajos. He says a person must understand and be aware of people's culture and lifestyles. "I was put in my place several times," he admits. "I've had to think things over because some people would tell me that it's done a certain way. You have to be sensitive to people's needs."

One test of this sensitivity is to know *when* it is appropriate to buy something from a traditional Navajo family. Some items are purchased only at certain times of year for specific seasonal ceremonies, such as the Yei bi cha (night chant) healing ceremony. (Buying deerskin in winter is one example.)

Dennis says it is also important to stay focused on the company's goals. For example, an artist may come in with several items to sell—pleading with buyers that he needs the money to make a car payment. "We try to get away from that. I've been here long enough to know who is really out there to make jewelry," he says.

"Being a controller in the accounting department, you might think that I would be here doing that—working with numbers," says Dennis. "But I take it upon myself to get out and learn about the merchandise we sell."

When Dennis was hired by Raymond Smith in 1991, he signed a three-year contract with the NACE board, agreeing to stay with the company until the accounting department was running smoothly and the entire department was equipped with computers. "In July of 1994, I went before the board and told them I wanted a four-year extension on my contract, because this is how long it's going to take to get everything rolling. They agreed with me and told me I was doing a great job."

Dennis, however, does not want to take all the credit for upgrading the accounting department. "It's everybody, people out on the floor and the branch managers, the buyers, Mr. Smith, the board members, and all those who are willing to work as a team. If it wasn't for them, their knowledge, and what they put into their stores, it could be lost."

plaques, including a nomination to the World Wide Global Business Leaders of America, a nationwide organization of auditors. "Our sales have been increasing at a steady pace over the past three years. We made quite a bit of profit last year, which is all pumped back into the company."

One way NACE serves tribal, public school, and federal health agency employees is to sell them arts and crafts on a payroll deduction plan—a NACE-operated credit system. This plan has expanded to about 3,500 customers who must be permanent employees of the tribal, state, or federal government. "As far as cash flow goes," explains Dennis, "it's

Charts, graphs, and reports are always being prepared.

one thing we really have to watch. The company doesn't receive payments for these purchases for about five to six months. That's one part of being a controller: trying to watch the cash flow and what we need to buy and where we spend the money. I try to maintain the appropriate level of cash flow."

The accounting staff keeps track of all NACE sales. The accounting department includes a senior accountant, two accountants, and two clerks. The senior accountant prepares daily cash journals and sales reports, pays bills, and creates credit plans for all the stores. The other accountants handle the company's payroll, assist the senior accountant in preparing sales journals, and count the cash every day. Among other duties, the clerks prepare authorizations for credit plan charges that are approved by Dennis.

As a member of the management team, Dennis takes it upon himself to learn about what is going on in the other departments. He is probably the only person at NACE who is not a craftsman. "I didn't know much about how some of these items were made or how much they cost. But I've learned an awful lot here," he says.

According to a 1992 report to the tribal council, NACE started showing a profit of $17,507 in 1990. Prior to this, the enterprise lost $51,335 a year. NACE's total 1990 sales were $3.1 million. At the end of 1992, the gross sales were $4 million with a profit of $446,602. "This is an indication that things are looking a lot better for us," says manager Raymond Smith.

NACE, like several other reservation enterprises, is owned by the tribal government, and this limits growth. "For example, we can't get a loan from any bank unless we get approval from the tribal council," Raymond says. "Even if we do get the approval it is a very slow process, because it goes through a number of committees and tribal officials before it reaches the tribal council."

Board chairman Frank Chee Willeto thinks things should change: "Personally, I think the business would be better off if it were to separate from the tribe. There are many things we can't do without them or without their approval. It's hard to work with, but we have been coping with it so far."

There are no formal plans to separate NACE from the tribe; however, there are plans for more expansion. Even under the present system NACE opened a store in August 1994 in the heart of Indian trader territory: Gallup, New Mexico.

In Gallup, NACE competes with many other stores for business.

· 4 ·

The Future of NACE

With the opening of the Gallup store, NACE has become a major player in the wholesale market.

"We felt we needed to be in the mainstream," says Russell Morgan, wholesale division manager. "Indian arts and crafts dealers come into Gallup to buy, because this town is known for its many arts and crafts businesses." Studies show that 90 percent of the Indian jewelry business is conducted in the border town of Gallup, New Mexico. "Border" towns are located off the reservation and offer commercial activity not available on the reservation: Malls, car dealerships, and other businesses often thrive in such towns. In 1989, Gallup generated $50 million in sales of Indian arts and crafts. NACE sold more than $2 million that year.

Russell says it's still too early to estimate how much money the Gallup store has made or how long it will take to make a profit. "We don't expect to make a profit for a couple of years," he says. "To be fair, I would expect [a profit] in about three years. NACE has a good future here [in Gallup] as far as the wholesale market goes. Retailers like to see Navajos here, and they would like to see more." So far, NACE is the only Navajo-owned arts and crafts store in Gallup.

The first step toward competing with Gallup and other border-town traders was the establishment of a NACE mobile sales office in 1986. NACE received a grant of $10,000 from the Bureau of Indian Affairs to study whether a mobile store operation would be successful. After finding that it would be, the enterprise was awarded a BIA grant and loan to purchase a

Thomas Burnside (left) and Jeffrey Morgan have the mobile store open and ready for business.

mobile store. Stocked with silver, turquoise, coral, wool, and thousands of other supplies and tools, the mobile store now travels throughout the reservation selling raw materials to crafts makers.

"The mobile store takes regular tours to distant places like Leupp [Arizona], Kayenta, Kaibito, and Shiprock [New Mexico]," says controller Dennis Wyna. "It's a service for people who live in isolated areas, so they don't have to travel long distances to purchase their materials."

As a retired silversmith, Frank Chee Willeto sees the benefits of using the mobile store to entice new customers as well as to get more exposure among the craftspeople who would normally travel to the border towns to buy their supplies. "Our mobile store is doing well. We feel that the silversmiths can

Customers drive up to the mobile store and find plenty of selection for the supplies they need.

make a little more money, or save a little more money, by not traveling far distances to get their supplies."

The second expansion move was to create a wholesale division of NACE. The difference between retail and wholesale is the amount of jewelry sold to individuals or companies. Retail sales are individual pieces sold to a customer. Wholesale purchases are large orders sold to either individuals or jewelry companies, who often then sell the jewelry to individuals in quantity—NACE will become a jewelry factory as it was years before.

Work on the new division started in January 1993 with four employees working on the technical details. The wholesale division works with the small town of Alamo, New Mexico, 250 miles southwest of Window Rock. The community was especially interested in the project because of its remote location. Many Alamo residents are skilled silversmiths who had to travel hundreds of miles to Albuquerque, New Mexico, to sell their crafts. A group of silversmiths from Alamo, New Mexico, approached NACE, the tribal government, and their own chapter government to see if an outlet would be built in Alamo for their use. You could say the wholesale division started at Alamo when individual silversmiths from the town were employed on a temporary basis to mass-produce the jewelry so they would no longer have to travel to Albuquerque to sell their work.

Russell Morgan supervises the work of the Alamo silversmiths and reports: "I don't like to use the word *manufacturing,* but for lack of a better term, we are producing top-quality jewelry using only quality sterling silver and turquoise," he says.

Russell has been with NACE for nearly eleven years. He was hired as an accountant and later transferred to the sales manager's position before the creation of the wholesale division. He has attended the University of New Mexico's business school. On top of that, he has more than twenty years' experience in the retail business both off and on the Navajo reservation.

The difference between other Indian jewelry businesses and NACE's Alamo mass production, Russell says, is in the actual making of the jewelry. Each piece of jewelry is individually handcrafted by one of fifty silversmiths who work from their homes.

"These silversmiths still maintain the authenticity of their work. It's not

RUSSELL MORGAN

Russell Morgan, forty-four, is the manager of NACE's wholesale division. He began working in the retail business in 1974, soon after he graduated from Window Rock High School and attended the University of New Mexico in Albuquerque for business administration.

Russell grew up around the Navajo Nation's capital. He watched the development of the tribal government and the local economic growth of the community. "I had been interested in the retail business ever since I can remember," Russell recalls. "The development and growth of businesses on the reservation has not been good until recently . . . [when] larger grocery stores and several fast-food chain stores have been built. I've always wanted to play a role in the growth and development of the reservation's economy."

Russell's first job in the retail business was for FedMart, one of the few large grocery and department stores on the reservation. "I worked in the department section of the store, where I was in charge of the electronics and sporting goods," he recalls. He stayed with that company for about nine years and briefly transferred to its headquarters in Phoenix, Arizona, to get experience outside the reservation. Eleven years ago he was hired by the Navajo Arts and Crafts Enterprise.

"When I first started, I worked as an accountant," he says. From accounting he moved to sales, and then became a sales manager. When NACE started its wholesale division, he was put in charge.

"With my experience in the retail industry," he says, "I had confidence that I could contribute to NACE's challenges of becoming a viable business. When I got here, there were very few employees who knew what was going on or what to do. I would like to think that some of my ideas and experiences have been my contributions throughout the years."

As manager of the wholesale division, Russell set up his own office and workshop at the Gallup, New Mexico, store in August of 1994. He supervises fifty silversmiths working from their homes in Alamo, six buffers, two salesclerks, and two traveling sales representatives.

"I don't really have a routine to follow," Russell says as he relaxes in his small office in the back of the store. This store is very contemporary: Neon lights advertise Indian jewelry, glass windows surround the entire front of the store facing the busy downtown streets of Gallup. "That's what I like about this business. Every day is not the same. Every two weeks I've got to go down to Alamo to meet with silversmiths and the branch manager. Daily business, it's always different. Customers coming in, meeting different people all the time, selling different products each day."

Russell lives in Fort Defiance, about five miles north of Window Rock. He has no plans to leave his current job. "I want to stay with this business [NACE] because I really believe in what we're doing and I'm really interested in seeing the products promoted. As Navajos, we have our own unique talents. I would like to see more exposure of Navajo arts and crafts in different parts of the world. I think we have something here that I like to share with other people."

Russell Morgan manages the silversmiths who work for the wholesale division.

an assembly line process," he says. NACE designs the jewelry and "the silversmiths are given packets [of raw materials] and can do the work at home or use the NACE facilities. They bring the finished items back to us. They are paid by each piece and are not on any contract; nor are they permanent employees of NACE."

Russell says a lot of the so-called Gallup jewelry is manufactured on assembly lines, where several people work on one piece to save time and money. "They still call it handmade Indian jewelry, because Navajo workers are employed to do the work. That's how they keep their costs down. Here, at NACE, we employ Navajo silversmiths to work from start to finish on each piece of work. We know the quality is there."

In late November 1993, NACE opened a store in Alamo. It's a renovated stone building that once was a school. The government of Alamo used its own money to renovate the building. The store has a retail section that, in addition to finished jewelry, sells raw materials such as silver, stones, and all types of tools needed for silversmithing and rug weaving. There are two separate rooms where silversmiths can work and a section where four people can buff and polish finished jewelry.

General manager Raymond Smith hopes that NACE's wholesale division will eventually be in a position to compete successfully within the national and international wholesale market.

Toward that end, Russell Morgan plans to publish and distribute a catalog that will display a 250-piece assortment of jewelry produced by the wholesale division. "We will be putting together a wholesale catalog to be distributed throughout the United States and other parts of the world."

NACE says its advantage in wholesale jewelry remains quality.

"We're doing very well, considering that we only started in January 1993," says Russell. "Our production is way ahead of schedule; saleswise, we're right on schedule. My number one goal is to be more competitive and get a larger share of the wholesale business in this industry. Based on retail value, we're probably grossing about $20,000 a week. Since January 1993, we've sold well over $1 million."

Roselyn Begay takes inventory of the wholesale division.

Russell also has two salespeople traveling around the country for the wholesale division. "We're getting an excellent response so far," he reports. "Everybody is really impressed by what we're doing—selling quality jewelry. Customers are really impressed with the variety and quality."

NACE's next expansions are in the planning stages: retail stores in Albuquerque, New Mexico; and in Flagstaff, Page, and Phoenix, Arizona. Studies show the competition would be fierce. Raymond Smith says the board also has considered the possibility of franchising its branch stores to Navajos

Ready for the competition—these turquoise stones are ready for setting into silver.

interested in owning their own businesses. NACE would then become their sole supplier.

Speaking for the board, Chairman Frank Chee Willeto predicts that the Indian jewelry business will continue to thrive. "The jewelry business will always be here, so why not join in the competition? We are capable of that."

Glossary

board of directors   a group of individuals who manage or control a business.

buff   to shine or polish.

cash flow   money coming into the business through sales.

chairman of the board   the person who presides over the entire board of directors.

competition   others who provide similar goods or services.

controller   the person who audits accounts and supervises financial affairs.

co-op   a cooperative. A group of organized artisans or community members who produce and market their crafts for sale to retailers or individual customers.

council delegate   an elected official of a tribal community or chapter.

franchising   permitting an individual or group to market a business's goods or services within a particular territory.

housing   the base of a piece of silver jewelry in which a stone or jewel is set.

loom   a large tool used to weave yarn into rugs.

mass-produce   to produce in large quantities.

raw materials   unfinished pieces (such as silver and turquoise) used to make products (such as jewelry).

reservation   public land set aside by the federal government for American Indians.

retail   the sale of products in small quantities to consumers.

sandpaintings   paintings created with sand.

solder   to join pieces of metal together with heat.

vendor   someone who sells.

wholesale   the sale of products in bulk or large quantities for resale by a retailer. Wholesale products typically cost less than retail products.

Appendix A

Crafts Associations

American Craft Council
40 W. 53rd St.
New York, NY 10019
(212) 956-3535

Indian Arts and Crafts Association
122 La Beta, N.E.
Albuquerque, NM 87108
(505) 265-9149

American Arts and Crafts Alliance
425 Riverside Dr., Apt. 15H
New York, NY 10025
(212) 866-2239

Jewelry Manufacturers Association
1430 Broadway, Suite 1603
New York, NY 10018
(212) 730-2900

Society of Craft Designers
6175 Barfield Rd., Suite 220
Atlanta, GA 30328
(404) 252-2454

Association of Crafts and Creative Industries
P.O. Box 2188
Zanesville, OH 43702-2188

Appendix B

American Indian Associations

Navajo Arts and Crafts Enterprise
P.O. Box 160
Window Rock, AZ 86515
(520) 871-4090

Office of the President
The Navajo Nation
Window Rock, AZ 86515
(520) 871-6352

Navajoland Tourism Department
The Navajo Nation
Window Rock, AZ 86515
(520) 871-6436

The Indian Trader
P.O. Box 1421
Gallup, NM 87108
(505) 722-8894

Office of Indian Affairs
State of New Mexico
LaVilla Rivera Building
Santa Fe, NM 87501

Center for American Indian Economic Development
Joan Timeche, Coordinator
Northern Arizona University
P.O. Box 15066
Flagstaff, AZ 86011
(520) 523-7320

Office of Indian Affairs
State of Arizona
1700 W. Washington
Phoenix, AZ 85007

Navajo Community College
Attn: Navajo Cultural Department
Tsaile, Arizona 86556
(520) 724-3311

Indian Pueblo Cultural Center
2401 12th Street, NW
Albuquerque, NM 87104
(505) 844-3820

American Indian Culture Research Center
Box 98
Blue Cloud Abbey
Marvin, SD 57251
(605) 432-5528

Indian Arts and Crafts Association
122 La Beta, N.E.
Albuquerque, NM 87108
(505) 265-9149

Institute of American Indian Arts
P.O. Box 20007
Santa Fe, NM 87504-0007
(505) 988-6463

National Indian Youth Council
318 Elm St., SE
Albuquerque, NM 87102
(505) 247-2251

North American Indian Museums Association
c/o Seneca Iroquois Natl. Museum
Allegany Indian Reservation
P.O. Box 442
Salamanca, NY 14779
(716) 945-1738

Organization of North American Indian Students
Box 26, University Center
Northern Michigan Univ.
Marquette, MI 49855
(906) 227-2138

National Native American Cooperative
P.O. Box 5000
San Carlos, AZ 85550
(602) 230-3399

Council for Native American Indian Progress
280 Broadway, Suite 316
New York, NY 10007

Institute for the Study of Traditional American Indian Arts
P.O. Box 66124
Portland, OR 97266
(503) 233-8131

Index